Bond's Cookbo

Recipes for the Spy in You

by

Betty Green

Copyright/License Page

Table of Contents

Introduction

It does not matter whether the terrorists are your wife or kids (no pun intended), James Bond is a classic movie personality, and his eccentric gentleman-ness caught our eyes. However, despite how he ate, this handsome hunk of deliciousness was the ladies' man, and his physique could make Adonis green with envy. Whether it's the look, style, or voice, we know one thing, he was a sucker for good food, and we have this on lockdown.

Based on a frictional series, James Bond was a crafty secret service agent with all the tools in his arsenal. When he first graced our screens in 1953, this friction created by Ian Fleming got us drooling for his good looks. James Bond held down this position for as long as we can remember, and although he later parted ways to relax, we will never forget the handsome spy that graced our screens. Ah, but that was not all. Later as the movies continue, we saw the creamy Daniel Craig and his chiseled looks fill that void, and Bond was revived in us. Well, as we watched these men, we also soaked in their taste for good food and delicious drinks, especially the Martinis.

So if you are ready, let's get into the kitchen with our spies and see just what made these men who they are. You know, even though these recipes look like everyday recipes, they have the Bond/007 touch and seal of approval. Are you ready to discover just what tickles the spy in you?

xxxxxxxxxxxxxxxxxxxxxxxxxxxxxxxxxxxxxxxx

Recipe 1: Beefsteak and Well-Cooked Spiced Chips

Spicy chip is a perfect way to start your day and combining it with beef steak makes it perfect.

Cooking Time: 60 minutes

Yield: 3

List of Ingredients:

- 2 big potatoes
- 1 cup of oil
- 6oz of beef steak
- 1/2 tsp. of salt
- 1/2 tsp. of ground black pepper

xxxxxxxxxxxxxxxxxxxxxxxxxxxxxxxxxxxxxxxx

How to Cook:

Peel your potatoes, slice nicely, wash and drain with a paper towel.

Heat up your oil in a deep pan and place your potatoes in the heated oil and allow it to fry until it is crispy.

Remove your tips from the oil and drain properly and allow it to cool. Fry it again until it turns golden brown, drain and sprinkle a little salt on it.

Poke your beef steak, sprinkle a little oil on it then grill it until the oil in it begins to come out. Season it with your pepper and grill for another 2 minutes.

Once it is cooked, set aside, to settle then you can serve it with your crispy chips and dijon mustard.

Recipe 2: Toasted French Bread

Taking you down to the French lane, this simple to make toast is one you cannot miss out on, it is unique and really tasty.

Cooking Time: 30minutes

Yield: 6

List of Ingredients:

- 4 large eggs
- 2 cups of milk
- 1 tsp. of salt
- 1 cup of flour
- 2 cups of sugar
- 1 tsp. of vanilla
- 1 tsp. of ground cinnamon
- 6 slices of French toast bread
- 2 tbsp. of butter
- 1 spoon of powdered sugar
- 1 spoon of butter and syrup.

xxxxxxxxxxxxxxxxxxxxxxxxxxxxxxxxxxxxxxxxx

How to Cook:

Whisk your eggs, milk, flour, sugar, vanilla, salt, and cinnamon together in a bowl.

Heat your pan and add your butter to it and allow it to heat. Dip your slice of bread one after the other into the oil.

Put in your pan and cook until it is golden brown.

Then your toast is ready to be served. You can serve with your butter and hot syrup to make it tastier.

Recipe 3: Stuffed Fried Mushroom

Prepare your mushroom in a way that will make you feel like an agent in 007. Prepare it the way Bond would love it, and your family will love it also. With this meal, you can resolve any grudge between you and anyone that will taste it.

Cooking Time: 40minutes

Yield: 8

List of Ingredients:

- 1 pack of sausage
- 1/2 cup of well-chopped onion
- 1 clove of minced garlic
- 1 pack of cream cheese
- 1/2 cup of shredded parmesan cheese
- 1 tsp. of dried parsley
- 1 tsp. of dried basil
- 1/2 cup of bread crumbs
- 20 pieces of big mushrooms
- 2 spoons of melted butter

xxxxxxxxxxxxxxxxxxxxxxxxxxxxxxxxxxxxxx

How to Cook:

Heat your oven first for over 300 degrees.

Cook your sausage, onion, and garlic for about 10minutes or cook until your sausage is well cooked. Shred your cooked sausage in crumbles and drain.

Add your cream cheese, and parmesan cheese and cook them until it is melted. Then add your basil, bread crumbs, and parsley.

Then put your mushroom in a greased baking pan, stem up, brush with butter, then put your sausage mixture into your mushroom cap and place in the oven. Let it bake till the mushrooms are tender.

Then serve your delicious mushrooms.

Recipe 4: Vesper Inspired Jambalaya Soup

Try our jambalaya soup and you will never regret it. It is unique and very tasty.

Cooking Time: 50 minutes

Yield: 6

List of Ingredients:

- 1 pack of your jambalaya mix
- 1 pack of smoked sausage
- 1 pound of shrimp
- 2 green onions
- 1 cup of shredded cheddar cheese
- 1/2 cup of pico and Gallo

XXXXXXXXXXXXXXXXXXXXXXXXXXXXXXXXXXXXX

How to Cook:

Your Jambalaya comes with instructions, so use the instructions and prepare your jambalaya mixture.

Add your sausage and shrimp and cook properly. Then remove from the heat and pour in your cheese, green onions, and pico then heat it up together.

Recipe 5: Potato-Apple flavored Roasted Chicken

It's always fun when you can prepare your chicken in more than one way. Here is a unique recipe for you to prepare with your family and you will definitely have fun doing it.

Cooking Time: 2hours30minutes

Yield: 8

List of Ingredients:

- 1 boneless chicken
- 1 cup of bread crumb
- 2 spoons of melted butter
- 1/2 spoon of herbs
- 1/2 tsp. of salt
- 1/2 tsp. of pepper
- 1oz of chicken broth
- 1 big and well-chopped onions
- 2pounds of potatoes
- 1 big slice of apple.

xxxxxxxxxxxxxxxxxxxxxxxxxxxxxxxxxxxxxx

How to Cook:

Place your boneless chicken on a roasting pan

Mix your bread crumbs, melted butter, salt, pepper, and herbs together in a bowl then spread it over your meat.

Put your diced onion in a pan, pour your chicken broth in the pan together with your onion, then bake in your oven for about 60minutes.

Add your potatoes, and bake for another 20minutes, till it is soft.

When your meat is well cooked, remove from the oven, then serve with your apple.

Recipe 6: Soft and Lovely Scrambled Delicious Egg

It is almost certain that you love eggs and must have had eggs in different ways, but the unique egg is one thing you will love to try. And knowing that Bond loves his egg this way will make you love it even more.

Cooking Time: 20minutes

Yield: 4

List of Ingredients:

- 6 big eggs
- 1/2 cup of evaporated milk
- 1/3 tsp. of salt
- 1/8 tsp. pepper
- 1 spoon of oil
- 1 tbsp. of your processed cheese sauce

xxxxxxxxxxxxxxxxxxxxxxxxxxxxxxxxxxxxxxx

How to Cook:

Break your eggs into a bowl and whisk, add your evaporated milk, your salt, and pepper, and whisk together.

Heat your pan and pour your oil inside to heat up a little.

Once your oil is hot enough, pour your egg mixture in the pan and put your cheese sauce also.

Stir your eggs until it is well fried, and make sure it is thick.

Once it's been confirmed that your egg is well cooked, you bring it down and your egg is ready to be served.

You can serve it together with anything you want to eat your eggs with.

Recipe 7: Wild Mushrooms in Chicken Sauce

Curling up with your family on the sofa and watching your favorite 007 show seem like a great way to end the night. But your night will not be complete without this unique dish, so try it out using the method and ingredients below.

Cooking Time: 60 minutes

Yield: 4

List of Ingredients:

- 50 gram of dried mushroom
- 1oz of chicken broth
- 200 gram of chestnut mushrooms
- 8 pieces of smoked bacon
- 2 tbsp. of butter
- 1 medium-sized chopped onion
- 200g of risotto rice
- 1 cup of white wine
- 50 gram of parmesan
- 1oz of tossed chicken, well grated
- 1 can of parsley.

xxxxxxxxxxxxxxxxxxxxxxxxxxxxxxxxxxxxxxx

How to Cook:

Soak your dried mushroom in boiled water for about 25 minutes and drain. Then nicely chop your soaked mushrooms and add your chestnut mushroom to it.

Put a little butter in a pan and fry your bacon, add your onion and fry also. When it is tender, add your mushrooms and cook until it is tender. Add your rice and stir continuously. Add your chicken broth and chicken, stir properly and let it cook.

Add your parsley, parmesan, and butter, and allow to rest a little. Bring the heat down completely, stir together and serve.

Recipe 8: Sunny-Side Up Prosciutto Egg Sandwich

If you love to have breakfast with your family, then this will serve as a perfect breakfast for you and your family. But you can still have this any time of the day, even during dinner and you will surely love it.

Cooking Time: 30minutes

Yield: 4

List of Ingredients:

- 5 big eggs
- 5 spoons of mayonnaise
- 1 clove of garlic. Well minced
- 5 slices of sourdough bread.
- 1 cup of fresh arugula
- 1 large tomato seed, well sliced
- 1 tsp. of salt
- 1 tsp. of pepper
- 1/2 slice of prosciutto.

xxxxxxxxxxxxxxxxxxxxxxxxxxxxxxxxxxxxxx

How to Cook:

Heat your nonstick pan over medium heat.

Break your eggs one after the other into the pan, then reduce your heat so your eggs don't get burnt.

Fry your eggs until the yolk thickens and the egg whites become solid. You can as well turn the egg if you wish.

Mix your mayonnaise and garlic together and spread them over your toast slices. Add your tomato, arugula, prosciutto, and your already fried eggs. Then sprinkle your salt and pepper on it to taste.

Your egg sandwich is ready to be served.

Recipe 9: Tomato-Bacon French Toasted Mushroom

Try our French toasted mushroom and enjoy over the 007 series and your family will always see you as their James Bond.

Cooking Time: 30 minutes

Yield: 3

List of Ingredients:

- 6 streaky bacon
- 150 gram of tomatoes
- 2 spoons of tomato chutney
- 150 gram of chestnuts
- 1 spoon of oil
- 1 egg
- 1 cup of milk
- 5 slices of white bread
- 3 tbsp. of butter

xxxxxxxxxxxxxxxxxxxxxxxxxxxxxxxxxxxxxx

How to Cook:

Pre-heat your oven to about 350°, then grill your bacon for 5 minutes and set aside.

Grill your cherry tomatoes also for 5 minutes. Mix it with your tomato chutney and also set aside.

Put a little oil in a frying pan and fry your mushrooms for 5 minutes and also keep aside.

Whisk your egg together with your milk in a bowl and add your bread slices in it and allow it to soak up.

Hear up your butter and fry your soaked bread in it for 10 minutes while turning it.

When it turns golden brown, bring it down, top your tomato mixture, mushrooms, and bacon on it, then serve while hot.

Recipe 10: British Cherry-Clam Chowder Soup

Everyone loves soup, and so does Bond. If you are hanging out with your family and watching the 007 series, you will likely want to prepare something quick and nice for them. Well, the chowder soup seems to be perfect and fast also.

Cooking Time: 60minutes

Yield: 8

List of Ingredients:

- 10 cherrystone clams
- 2 cups of cold water
- 1 bacon strip, well diced
- 1 onion, chopped
- 2 medium-sized potatoes. peel them and chop nicely.
- 2 tbsp. of flour
- 1/2 tsp. of pepper
- 1/2 tsp. of salt
- 1 cup of milk
- 1/2 cup of cream

xxxxxxxxxxxxxxxxxxxxxxxxxxxxxxxxxxxxxxxx

How to Cook:

Put your clams in a pot and add water to it and allow it to boil, until the clams open. Discard any clam that doesn't open.

Remove the meat from the clams and chop them nicely, then keep it aside.

Cook your diced bacon in a pan and cook it until it is crispy. Remove your bacon from the pan and put on a paper towel to drain the oil. Then soak up your diced onion in oil until it is soft.

Return your bacon to your pan, add your meat, and water. Add your potatoes, salt, and pepper to taste. Reduce the heat and cover your pan, allow it to boil until the potatoes are soft.

Mix your milk and flour together, then add it to your potato soup, cook until it is thick then you bring it down. Your soup is ready to be served.

Recipe 11: Canapes Dressed Shellfish

Having a meal of shellfish is always amazing and this is surely different from the usual shellfish you have in a seaside restaurant. What makes this unique is the fact that it will be prepared and served straight from your kitchen and it is fast food.

Cooking Time: 10 minutes

Yield: 4

List of Ingredients:

- 200 gram of white crabmeat
- 3 tbsp. of mayonnaise
- 1 tsp. of dijon mustard
- 2 tbsp. of lemon juice
- 1 tsp. of ground black pepper

XXXXXXXXXXXXXXXXXXXXXXXXXXXXXXXXXXXXX

How to Cook:

Mix your white crabmeat together with your mayonnaise, dijon mustard, lemon juice, salt, and black pepper to taste.

Put in your refrigerator to chill, then it is ready to be served.

Serve with your lettuce leaves arranged in the form of a cup and watch your family devour it hungrily.

Recipe 12: Slow Irish Potato Soup

Do you wish to enjoy watching your James Bond series with your family in the evening over a bowl of soup? And you are wondering what type of soup to preparing, we are here to help you. Try this unique Irish potato soup recipe and become an agent in your kitchen just like Mr. Bond.

Cooking Time: 5hours

Yield: 6

List of Ingredients:

- 1 carton of chicken broth
- 1 pack of frozen shredded Irish potatoes,
- 1 medium-sized
- 1 clove of minced garlic
- 1/2 tsp. of pepper
- 1 pack of cream cheese
- 1/2 cup of cream
- 1/2 cup of shredded cheddar cheese

xxxxxxxxxxxxxxxxxxxxxxxxxxxxxxxxxxxxxxx

How to Cook:

Mix your chicken broth, potatoes, onion, garlic, salt, and pepper together in a slow cooker and allow it to cook on low heat for about 5hours.

Mix your cheese cream properly until it is melted. Mash your potatoes properly,

Cook them together for about 10 minutes then pour into your chicken broth and allow it to cook properly.

When it is well cooked, you can bring it down and your soup is ready to be served.

Recipe 13: Spicy Chili-Parsley Crab

Crab is a nutritious seafood and everyone loves to eat healthily, so try our latest crab recipe right in your kitchen, and have fun devouring the delicious and tasty spicy crab.

Cooking Time: 30minutes

Yield: 4

List of Ingredients:

- 200 gram of linguine
- 4 tbsp. of oil
- 1 piece of red chili, well diced
- 1 clove of minced garlic
- 1 big crab
- 2oz of brown crabmeat
- 5oz of white crabmeat
- 4 spoons of white wine
- 1 spoon of lemon zest
- 1 cup of fresh parsley leaf

xxxxxxxxxxxxxxxxxxxxxxxxxxxxxxxxxxxxxxx

How to Cook:

Put salt water in a cooking pan and allow it to boil then you add your linguine. Stir continuously while it is boiling so it doesn't get too thick.

While your linguine is cooking, heat up 3 spoons of your oil together with your chili and garlic, let it cook properly until it simmers then you turn down the heat.

Add your white wine and mix properly with your oil, then add your brown crabmeat, mash it together with your chili mixture to make a thick sauce.

When your linguine is tender, bring it down and put your saucepan on low heat. Add your linguine in your mashed mixture, add your white crabmeat, and parsley leaf, mix properly, sprinkle a little salt. Stir properly and if it's getting too thick, you can add a little of your linguine water and stir.

Add your lemon zest, stir together and serve your yummy and tasty spicy crab.

Recipe 14: Bond and Vesper Inspired Glazed Lamb Stake

In one of the 007 series, Bond and Vesper had a serious argument, but they ended up settling their disagreement over a plate of glazed lamb. Hence, this particular recipe is inspired by them.

Cooking Time: 40 minutes

Yield: 8

List of Ingredients:

- 1 can of cranberry sauce
- 1 tbsp. of brown sugar
- 2 tsp. of chili powder
- 1 spoon of garlic powder
- 1/2 spoon of paprika
- 1 tsp. of salt
- 1 pound of a lamb without bone.

xxxxxxxxxxxxxxxxxxxxxxxxxxxxxxxxxxxxxx

How to Cook:

Mix your cranberry sauce, Brian sugar, chili powder, salt, garlic, and paprika together in a bowl.

Add your lamb to the mixture and cover it for hours or overnight to marinade.

Remove your lamb from the marinade, then weave the lamb onto your wooden stake, arrange in a foil and put in your baking pan, allow it to bake for about 3minutes.

Make a sauce from your remaining cranberry sauce and serve alongside your lamb.

Recipe 15: Spy Snickerdoodle Toast

Another type of toast inspired by your favorite 007 series. No need going out to enjoy this specialty, prepare it right from your kitchen and enjoy in the comfort of your home.

Cooking Time: 30minutes

Yield: 4

List of Ingredients:

- 2 cups of milk
- 4 big eggs
- 1/2 tsp. of salt
- 1/2 tsp. of vanilla extract
- 5 slices of bread
- 1 cup of white sugar
- 2 tsp. of cinnamon

xxxxxxxxxxxxxxxxxxxxxxxxxxxxxxxxxxxxxxx

How to Cook:

Mix your cinnamon and sugar together and place aside.

Over low heat, heat up your frying pan

Mix your eggs, vanilla extract, salt, together. Then pour it into a large bowl.

Dip your bread slices in your mixture, poke with your fork so the mixture gets in.

Sprinkle one side of the bread with your cinnamon and sugar mixture and place it in your already heated pan.

Cook until it is golden brown, firm and not wet anymore. Then you can serve your toast with anything nice by the side.

Recipe 16: Bond Oyster Soup

This oyster soup is delicious and has a unique recipe that you would love. You must not miss out on this one as Bond loves oysters but he missed out on it before and it is certain he will love to have it in the comfort of his home.

Cooking Time: 90minutes

Yield: 4

List of Ingredients:

- 1 dozen of fresh oysters in the shell.
- 1 medium-sized onion, well chopped
- 1/2 cup of cubed butter
- 1 pack of fresh spinach
- 1/2 cup of romano cheese, grated.
- 1 spoon of like juice
- 1/2 tsp. of pepper
- 1tsp. of kosher salt

xxxxxxxxxxxxxxxxxxxxxxxxxxxxxxxxxxxxxxxx

How to Cook:

Remove your oysters from the shell and set aside.

Put your butter in a pan and your onions and fry until it is tender, then add your spinach and cook together

Remove it from the heat, add your cheese, lime juice, and pepper.

Spread your kosher salt into a baking pan that is not greased, press your oyster shells into the salt, then place an oyster each on top of the shell. Then top it with your spinach.

Bake everything together in your oven until your oysters become plump, then serve immediately while it is still hot.

Recipe 17: Baked Flavored French Fries

Taste your French fries on a whole new level. Using our unique recipe to prepare this will turn you into an agent in your kitchen, and a very smart one at that.

Cooking Time: 40minutes

Yield: 4

List of Ingredients:

- 4 pieces of potatoes
- 2 tbsp. of oil
- 1 tsp. of salt

xxxxxxxxxxxxxxxxxxxxxxxxxxxxxxxxxxxxxxxxxx

How to Cook:

Peel your potatoes and slice them in form of chips, put in a bowl and add water to it.

Wash out the starch and drain properly.

Mix your potatoes in your oil and sprinkle salt on it.

Grease your cookie sheet and spread your potatoes on it

Bake in your oven until it is crispy and serve while hot. You can serve with a barbeque fish or egg.

Recipe 18: Chocolate Cookies

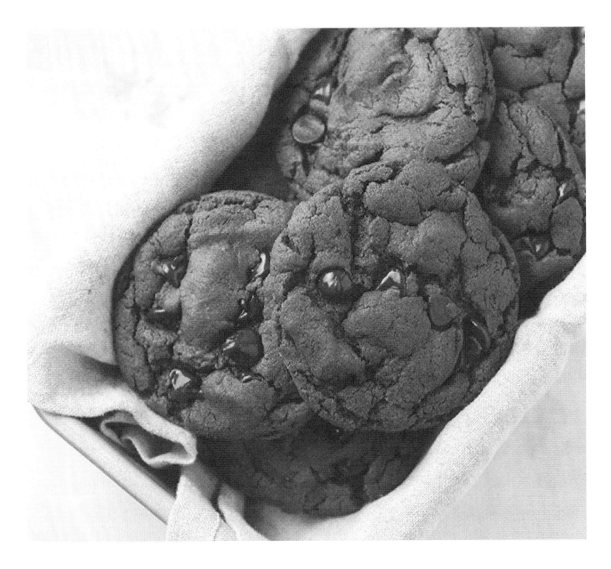

Looking for a quick snack to snack on during movie time with your family, then our favorite chocolate cookies are always great.

Cooking Time: 30minutes

Yield: 6

List of Ingredients:

- 2 cups of soft butter
- 2 tsp. of baking powder
- 2 cups of flour
- 1 cup of sugar
- 1 cup of brown sugar
- 5 big eggs
- 1 spoon of vanilla extract
- 1 tsp. of baking soda
- 1/2 tbsp. of salt
- 1 cup of cornflakes
- 1 cup of rolled oat
- 1 pack of shredded coconut
- 1 pack of chocolate chips
- 1/2 cup of diced walnuts

xxxxxxxxxxxxxxxxxxxxxxxxxxxxxxxxxxxxxxx

How to Cook:

Mix your butter and sugar in a bowl. Whisk your eggs and vanilla together and add to the bowl, combine the flour, baking powder, soda, and salt together. Then add it to your mixture and mix properly.

Add your cornflakes, oat, and shredded coconut, then add your chocolate chips and walnuts together.

Shape your mixture into balls and put in a tight container and separate the layers with wax paper, then put in the refrigerator all night.

Bake your balls in your oven for about 15minutes, until it is golden brown, then remove it to cool before you serve.

Recipe 19: Herndon Jelly-Filled Cake Donut

You've always had your cake and donut separately, but this recipe will let you in on how you can have both your cake and donut at the same time.

Cooking Time: 70minutes

Yield: 6

List of Ingredients:

- 1/2 cup of sugar
- 1 tsp. of ground cinnamon
- 1/2 tbsp. of salt
- 1/2 tsp. of ground nutmeg
- 1 cup of unsalted butter
- 2 eggs
- 1 cup of milk
- 1 spoon of sour cream
- 1 spoon of vanilla extract
- 2 cups of flour
- 1 tbsp. of baking powder
- 1 cup of strawberry jelly

xxxxxxxxxxxxxxxxxxxxxxxxxxxxxxxxxxxxxx

How to Cook:

Heat up your oven first. Then grease your pan and sprinkle flour on it also.

Put your sugar, cinnamon, salt, and nutmeg in a blender and blend. Transfer to a bowl, add your egg, butter, milk, sour cream, and vanilla extract and mix properly.

Mix your baking powder, and flour in another bowl and mix together with your sugar mixture.

Pour part of your batter in a pan, put your strawberry jelly in the middle, insert a toothpick and bake in your oven until the toothpick comes out clean. Bring it out and allow it to cool.

Mix your frosting ingredients in a bowl and spread over your cake. Sprinkle your cinnamon and sugar then refrigerate it for about 30 minutes and serve while cool.

Recipe 20: Fluffy Chocolate Cupcakes

Do you wish to become an agent in the kitchen? Then try our fluffy chocolate cupcakes for dessert and your family will adore you like the favorite James Bond.

Cooking Time: 40minutes

Yield: 6

List of Ingredients:

- 2 cups of flour
- 2 cups of baking cocoa
- 1 tbsp. of baking soda
- 1 cup of unsweetened coconut milk that has been refrigerated
- 1 cup of sugar
- 1/2 cup of oil
- 2 tbsp. of vinegar
- 1 spoon of vanilla extract
- 1 cup of margarine.

xxxxxxxxxxxxxxxxxxxxxxxxxxxxxxxxxxxxxxxx

How to Cook:

Heat your oven to about 360 degrees

Whisk your flour, cocoa, and baking soda in a large bowl, then mix your coconut milk, sugar, oil, vinegar, and vanilla extract in a separate bowl, then pour into your dry ingredients, mix until it is moistened.

Fill your muffin cup with your mixture. Put in your oven and allow it to bake for about 20minutes. You can insert a toothpick in the middle while baking, then when the toothpick comes out, your chocolate cupcake will be ready

Allow it to cool before serving, you can also frost your cupcake using your margarine to enjoy it better.

Recipe 21: Melina Inspired Grilled Figs

The grilled fig is a romantic recipe inspired by Melina in the 007 series. You can always prepare this unique recipe and enjoy it with your loved ones.

Cooking Time: 70 minutes

Yield: 5

List of Ingredients:

- 1 tsp. of sugar
- 1 tsp. of yeast
- 1/2 spoon of salt
- 1 cup of flour
- 1 cup of water
- 1 spoon of oil
- 1 pack of cream cheese
- 1/2 cup of honey
- 1/2 spoon of ground cinnamon
- 1 cup of dried fig.

xxxxxxxxxxxxxxxxxxxxxxxxxxxxxxxxxxxxxxx

How to Cook:

Mix your sugar, yeast, salt, and flour in a bowl. Then heat your water and oil in a saucepan and add it to your mixture. Then whisk together, then pour in your remaining flour and stir till its thick and sticky.

Turn your mixture onto a floured surface and mix until it is smooth and like an elastic. Put it in a bowl that is greased, turn it then cover to rise.

Knead your dough again and roll it into a ball, put in a foil and refrigerate.

Mix your cream cheese, honey, and ground cinnamon in a smaller bowl. Put your dough in the oven and grill for about 5minutes, bring it out and top your cinnamon mixture and dried fig then return it back to the oven, heat until it is golden brown then your Melina inspired fig is ready to be served.

It's better served hot, relax and enjoy it with your loved one.

Recipe 22: Cucumber Beluga Carpers

This is a delicacy that you and your family would love and topping it on your cucumber will make it more appetizing and delicious.

Cooking Time: 30minutes

Yield: 5

List of Ingredients:

- 1/2 cup of mayonnaise
- 2 ounces of soft cheese cream
- 1 spoon of grated onion
- 1 tsp. of minced chives
- 1/2 tsp. of vinegar
- 1 tsp. of Worcestershire sauce
- 1 clove of minced garlic
- 1/2 tsp. of paprika
- 1/2 tsp. of curry powder
- 1/2 tsp. of dried oregano
- 1/2 tsp. of thyme, and basil
- 1/2 tsp. of parsley
- 1 pound of white bread
- 2 big cucumbers
- 1 spoon of diced pimento

xxxxxxxxxxxxxxxxxxxxxxxxxxxxxxxxxxxxxx

How to Cook:

Put your mayonnaise, vinegar, cheese, onion, chives, garlic, Worcestershire sauce, and seasoning in your food processor and blend. Then put in a bowl, cover, and refrigerate it for about one hour.

Cut out circles from your bread, then circulate your mixture over the bread, add your cucumber slices and garnish with your pimento and dill. Then your carper is ready to be served.

Recipe 23: Hotdog Pizza

Pizza is always nice to have with the family but having it in a different way is totally mesmerizing.

Cooking Time: 60 minutes

Yield: 6

List of Ingredients:

- 1 ounce of hotdog
- 1 pack of pizza dough
- 1/2 cup of pizza sauce
- 2 cups of shredded cheese
- 1 small-sized
- 1 green pepper
- 1 cup of sliced mushroom
- 1 spoon of parmesan cheese
- 1 spoon of red pepper flakes

xxxxxxxxxxxxxxxxxxxxxxxxxxxxxxxxxxxxxxxxx

How to Cook:

Divide your pizza dough into two parts, oil your fingers and put each on your pizza pan.

Pinch the dough with a fork and allow it to bake until it gets lightly brown.

Cook your sausage until it is well cooked and drain it. Spread your pizza sauce over your dough, add your cheese, onion, green pepper, sausage, and mushroom, then bake until your cheese is bubbling.

You can also add your pepper flakes and parmesan cheese and your spicy hotdog pizza is ready to be served.

Recipe 24: Chicken Dip

Having to eat your chicken in different ways always tastes better than the regular. Try out our unique chicken dip recipe and you will love it.

Cooking Time: 30 minutes

Yield: 4

List of Ingredients:

- 1 pound of boneless chicken
- 1 cup of wing sauce
- 1 pack of soft cream cheese
- 1/2 cup of salad dressing
- 1/2 cup of sour cream
- 1 cup of shredded cheese
- 2 tbsp. of crumbled cheese
- 1 green onion bulb
- 1oz of tortilla chips

xxxxxxxxxxxxxxxxxxxxxxxxxxxxxxxxxxxxxxxx

How to Cook:

Put your chicken, wing sauce, and cream cheese in a pressure cooker pot and allow it to cook for about 10minutes.

Then remove your chicken, shred it, and stir in your cream cheese, salad dressing, sour cream, and your cheddar cheese. , sprinkle it with your leftover cheddar cheese, diced green onion, and blue cheese.

Then your chicken dip is ready to be served. You can serve with your tortilla chips or anything by the side.

Recipe 25: Grilled Peppered Mushroom

James Bond is great at his job no doubt and he acted well as an agent in the 007 series, so you too can be an agent in your kitchen and prepare our unique grilled peppered mushroom.

Cooking Time: 30 minutes

Yield: 5

List of Ingredients:

- 1 tbsp. of butter
- 1 cup of fresh mushroom
- 1 clove of minced garlic
- 2 whole fillets
- 1/2 tsp. of paprika
- 1/2 spoon of lemon/pepper seasoning
- 1 spoon of cayenne pepper
- 1 medium-sized well-chopped tomato
- 2 green sliced onions

xxxxxxxxxxxxxxxxxxxxxxxxxxxxxxxxxxxxxxx

How to Cook:

Heat your butter over low heat, add your mushrooms in your heated butter and cook until it is tender. Add your garlic and cook a bit longer.

Place your whole fillets on your mushroom, sprinkle your paprika, lemon/pepper seasoning, and cayenne.

Cook for about 15minutes, sprinkle your tomato and green onions. Then your peppered mushroom is ready to be served.

Recipe 26: Vanilla Flavored Cupcake

The vanilla flavored cupcake is just perfect for a family gathering. It's always nice to have something different most times. This is different and unique so try it out in your kitchen.

Cooking Time: 50minutes

Serve: 4

List of Ingredients:

- 2 cups of soft butter
- 1 cup of milk
- 2 tsp. of baking powder
- 1 cup of sugar
- 2 big eggs
- 1/2 tbsp. of salt
- 2 cups of flour
- 1/2 spoon of xanthan gum
- 1 pack of soft cream cheese
- 1 tsp. of vanilla extract
- 2 cups of confectioner's sugar

xxxxxxxxxxxxxxxxxxxxxxxxxxxxxxxxxxxxxx

How to Cook:

Heat up your oven before time

Cream your butter and sugar together until it's very light and fluffy. Add your eggs, and vanilla extract and mix properly.

Mix your flour, baking powder, xanthan gum, and salt in another bowl. Then add it to your wet mixture, add milk, and mix properly.

Fill your muffin cakes with your mixture, put in the oven and bake for about 20 minutes, until your cakes out golden brown and well baked.

Bring out your cupcakes and allow it to cool before serving. Serve with your whisked vanilla, milk, and confectionery sugar as frost on the cupcake.

Recipe 27: Rice with Shrimp Soup

Try our unique shrimp soup recipe served with rice, you will feel like you are Bond himself while preparing the meal.

Cooking Time: 40 minutes

Serve: 4

List of Ingredients:

- 2 tbsp. of butter
- 2 celery ribs
- 1 small diced onion
- 1/2 cup of lemon juice
- 4 cloves of minced garlic
- 1 spoon of sugar
- 1 can of diced tomato
- 1 pound of cooked shrimp
- 4 ounces of tomato paste
- Boiled rice

xxxxxxxxxxxxxxxxxxxxxxxxxxxxxxxxxxxxxxxxx

How to Cook:

Heat your butter over slightly medium heat, add your celery and onions in your heated butter and cook until it is crispy.

Add your lemon juice, garlic, and sugar; cook a little more, then transfer to a slow cooker and let it cook slowly. Add your tomato paste, your juice, shrimp, and cook. Then you can serve your shrimp with your already boiled rice.

Recipe 28: British styled Oven Baked Chicken

Another unique and fast food recipe that tastes very nice. Try this recipe and your family will love you much more.

Cooking Time: 60minutes

Yield: 4

List of Ingredients:

- 1 cup of Ritz crackers
- 1 spoon of fresh parsley
- 1/2 spoon of garlic salt
- 1 tsp. of paprika
- 1/2 spoon of pepper
- 1/2 tsp. of ground cumin
- 1/2 tsp. of sage
- 2 big eggs
- 2 pounds of chicken

xxxxxxxxxxxxxxxxxxxxxxxxxxxxxxxxxxxxxxxxx

How to Cook:

Heat up your oven, then coat your baking pan with cooking spray

Mix your parsley, crackers, paprika, garlic salt, pepper, cumin, and sage in a bowl. Then whisk your eggs in another bowl.

Dip your chicken in the eggs, then in the cracker mixture, pat it and place it in your baking pan.

Put in your oven and bake for about 20minutes, then turn the chicken. Allow it to bake properly until it is golden brown.

Then your oven-baked chicken is ready to be served.

Recipe 29: Curry-Coconut Flavored Shrimp

Instead of having your favorite shrimp in a restaurant, you can actually prepare it in your kitchen using our unique recipe and make your family excited while watching the 007 series.

Cooking Time: 30 minutes

Yield: 4

List of Ingredients:

- 2 cups of coconut milk
- 1 spoon of fish sauce
- 1 tsp. of curry powder
- 1/2 tsp. of brown sugar
- 1/2 tsp. of salt
- 1/2 tsp. of pepper
- 1 pack of shrimp
- 1 medium-sized red pepper, well chopped
- 1 bulb of green onions
- 1/2 cup of fresh cilantro
- 1 cup of jasmine rice
- 1 spoon of lime juice

xxxxxxxxxxxxxxxxxxxxxxxxxxxxxxxxxxxxxxx

How to Cook:

Mix your coconut milk, fish sauce, curry powder, brown sugar, salt, and pepper in a bowl.

Fry your shrimp in a frying pan using your mixture until the shrimp turns pink. Then remove from heat and allow it to cool a little.

Add your red pepper, onions, and your leftover mixture to the pan then allow it to boil.

Add your shrimp, and cilantro and heat together.

Then serve with your jasmine rice and garnish with your lime juice.

Recipe 30: Lamb Biscuit Skillet

You must have had something like this while growing up. It's time to remember your childhood and feel like the perfect kitchen agent for your kids.

Cooking Time: 30 minutes

Yield: 5

List of Ingredients:

- 1 spoon of butter
- 1/2 cup of diced onions
- 1 cup of flour
- 1oz of chicken broth
- 1/2 cup of milk
- 1/2 tsp. of pepper
- 1 cup of chicken breast
- 10oz of frozen peas and carrots
- 10 ounce of buttermilk biscuit

xxxxxxxxxxxxxxxxxxxxxxxxxxxxxxxxxxxxxxxx

How to Cook:

First, heat up your oven to about 350°. Then melt your butter in a skillet over mild heat, then add your onions and fry until it's tender.

Mix your flour, chicken broth, milk, and pepper until it is well mixed. Put it in a pan and let it boil, stir continuously until it is thick.

Add your peas, carrot, and lamb, and heat it up. Arrange your biscuits over your stew then heat until your biscuit turns golden brown.

Then serve your delicious lamb biscuit when it cools.

Conclusion

James Bond might be filled with action but he loves to have good food when he has the opportunity to eat. So in as much as you love to sit and watch him and all his series, you also need to become an agent in the kitchen by preparing our unique delicacy. This book is a combination of both the main dish and dessert, so have fun with your loved ones with our ingredients.

Announcement

Thank you very much for getting this book. By buying my book you show me that you are ready to learn new skills and I can tell for sure you have made the best decision. I become a recipe writer because I love to share my knowledge and experience so that other people can learn.

What's even more special is that from all the books that are available on the internet today you have mine. With every purchase done it's like a gift to me, proof that I've made the best decision, turning my experience and knowledge into a book.

Still, please do not forget to leave feedback after reading the book. This is very important for me because I'll know how far I have reached. Even if you have any suggestions that you think it will make my future books even more practice please do share. Plus, everyone else that won't be able to decide which book to get next will have real feedback to read.

Thank you again

Your truly

Betty Green

About the Author

The one thing she loves more than cooking is eating. Yes, Betty Green enjoys tasting new dishes and loves to experiment with food. While sticking to the classics is also a thing, she wants to create recipes that people can enjoy daily.

She really understands the struggle of choosing the next lunch or dinner or what they should serve at their parties. So, she makes sure that her recipes are not only great for family dinners, or even a single dish but for parties too.

She always says "I have a strong sense of smell and taste, which gives me an advantage in creating new recipes from scratch".

The best part of Betty's recipes is that they are practical and very easy to make. When she does use ingredients that are not so easy to find or rarely used in cooking she makes sure to explain everything and add a simplified cooking description so that everyone can make them.

Everyone who got a cookbook from her says that she changed their life. Helped them finally enjoy spending time in the kitchen, which even helped them bond stronger with their family and friends.

Well, after all, food is one of the best ways to connect with people whether they make the dish together or they sit down and eat it. There are countless ways food can help you in your life, aside from keeping you fed and healthy.

Printed in Great Britain
by Amazon